W9-BMO-259

Silly Sticker Stories™
Christmas Tales

HIGHLIGHTS PRESS

Honesdale, Pennsylvania

Create your own silly story!

Each Hidden Pictures® puzzle in this book comes with a story for you to finish. Use the tear-out sticker sheets to start puzzling!

Here's what you do:

1 Find a hidden object.

2 Peel the sticker.

A Day at the Beach
pages 4–5

The Perfect Tree
pages 6–7

Loco for Cocoa
pages 8–9

Choo-Choo on This
pages 10–11

Tear out sticker sheet here.

for Children, Inc.

magnifying glass
mitten
spoon
frying pan
banana
mallet
dog bone
snake
toothbrush
ruler
pencil
heart
bread
coat hanger
bell
candy kiss
turtle
envelope
chef's hat
peanut
green bean
moon
game piece
yo-yo
saltshaker
magnifying glass
pennant
seashell
ring
canoe
necklace
flowerpot
key
pie
saw

A Day at the Beach

"Even elves need a break," sa_____ _____ [spoon] produc_____

True, the elves have been stressed o__ this year, and a few did seem to be losing focus. Last week, I saw Binky trying to attach handlebars to a fluffy stuffed _____! So I hitched my team to the double-wide _____ and we all flew off to the beach before The Big Day. I had trouble relaxing until I saw Twinkle and Tony building a two-story-high _____ out of the soft _____. That made me smile! Even Dancer, Blitzen, and Rudolph the Red-Nosed _____ enjoyed zooming through the salty _____ rather than the starry _____ for a change. And who doesn't feel better after a big scoop of mint-chocolate _____? Back at the North _____, I'm going to give my wife an extra Christmas gift (a snorkeling _____) for giving me such a great idea!

BONUS: Can you find the fishhook and saw?

4

Art by Neil Numberman

Contents

3

Place it in the story.

4

Read aloud and giggle!

A Day at the Beach

"Even elves need a break," said my wife while I was overseeing

the production in my airplane-hangar-size _model_.

True, the elves have been stressed-out this year, and a few did seem

to be losing focus. Last week, I saw Binky trying to attach handlebars

to a fluffy stuffed _bear_! So I hitched my team to the double-

wide _sleigh_ and we all flew off to the beach before The Big

Day. I had trouble relaxing until I saw Twinkle and Tony building

a two-story-high _workshop_ out of the soft _sand_. That

made me smile! Even Dancer, Blitzen, and Rudolph the Red-Nosed

reindeer enjoyed zooming through the salty _water_ rather

than the starry _night_ for a change. And who doesn't feel

better after a big scoop of mint chocolate _Hot coaco_? Back at the

North _Pole_, I'm going to give my wife an extra Christmas

gift (a snorkeling _suit_) for giving me such a great idea!

BONUS: Can you find the fishhook and saw? ✔

Art by Neil Numberman

The Perfect Tree

Every year we head out to the Beck's Holiday _tree_ Farm

looking for the freshest, tallest _X-mas tree_ we can find. We walk

up and down, checking out each green, sweet-smelling _tree_.

We shake each prickly _vine_ to check that not even one

pointy _needle_ falls off. This year, Mom spotted one she liked

right away. "How about this one? It has the perfect shape, like an

equal-sided _doughnut_." I shook my head. "See that big, open

spot in the back? It looks as if a hungry _goblin_ took a

bite out of it." Another had clumps of brown spots, like an overripe

apple. Finally, we found one that everyone agreed on. Dad

cut it down with his trusty old _saw_, which is as sharp as a

ninja's _sword_. As we carried our final choice slowly up the

steep, snowy _hill_ to the car, I said, "Yep, we picked the

most perfect—oh, wait. What about that one?"

Art by Dana Regan

Loco for Cocoa

My school hosts a fundraiser that is the tastiest idea ever: a Hot

choclate Contest. It's a delicious way to earn money to send

our marching _band_ to the state championships every year.

We all have our favorite recipes. Some use _white_ milk and

float a puffy _marshmellow_ on top or dust with _cheese_ powder.

Others stir each serving with a striped _____ for a hint of

mint. My concoction uses a super secret ingredient: just a pinch or

two of cayenne _____! (It gives my entry a kick like a long-

eared _____ that's been tickled with a _____.) We had

the usual crowd, but then an unexpected group arrived. The guy

in the fancy red _____ marched right over to my table and

picked up a big, steaming _____ and gulped it down. I tried to

stop him, but it was too late. I heard him exclaim as he ran toward

the _____ fountain: "Now THAT was ho-ho-ho-HOT!"

BONUS: Can you find the banana and tack?

Art by David Helton

football

Choo-Choo on This

"All aboard the *choo choo* Express!" I called out. I never thought

I'd ever get the chance to live my dream: driving a steam-powered

train. But now I can! I take my job very seriously. Every morning,

I polish the _engine_ until it shines like a fancy _cookie_ glittering

in the sun. Nothing makes me feel more proud than putting the striped

hat on my head before I climb into the _driver_'s seat.

I always check my ~~watch~~ _trusty_ watch to be sure I start my route

on time. Though the clackety _tracks_ only goes around in a

circle, I get to see interesting sights such as the _not_ -wrapped

Mountains and the _pretty_ -decked Forest. I love blasting the

horn loudly to warn anyone trying to cross my path. So far, I've

only had one passenger—Mr. Bearnard. But he seems to enjoy the ride.

He always has the biggest, widest _smile_ on his face!

BONUS: Can you find the crown?

Art by Tim Davis

Home Sweet Home

You don't get an invitation like this every day: "Come

on down to the local _North pole_ mall and build a life-size

gingerbread house!" I knew that this was a sweet project that

I could really sink my _head_ into. So I couldn't wait to get

there with my mom and my dad and my pesky little _sister_.

First, I had to put a checkerboard-patterned ~~tablecloth~~ _clothes_ on

so my clothes wouldn't get messy. Then I was told to cover my

hands with a plastic _gloves_, reach into a white pail to

grab a gooey glob of _royal icing_, and slather it on the nearest

wall. (It took all my willpower not to lick my fingers.) The

last step was to take each spicy _piece_ and press it into the

soft, sticky _icing_. The best part? If a crumbly _part_

happened to break (by accident, of course), I could gobble it up!

Mmmm... For once, I didn't mind making a mistake!

BONUS: Can you find the bunch of grapes, envelope, golf club, comb, and teacup?

Art by Neil Numberman

A-Caroling We Go!

We had been practicing for weeks. It's an old _good_-family

tradition to go door-to-_door_ and treat our neighbors to a

tuneful _caroling_. Spot and I sometimes argue over which of us

is the most amazing _singer_ ever. I think his _sound_ is low

and gravelly, and sounds like an old _car_ bumping along a

dirt _road_. Of course, my much more musical _voise_

is high and sweet, like a chocolate-chip _cookie_ stored in a

twelve-foot-tall _cobord_. But we agree that, together, we make

everyone sit back on their hind legs and take notice. So when we

arrived at the Petersons' house on our block, we couldn't wait to

belt out the beloved _song_ that we had rehearsed. Everyone

else began crooning "Hark! the herald angels sing," but then stopped

and stared when we joined in. Oops! Did they say "hark"? We

thought the first word of the song was "_back_"!

Art by Pat Lewis

Winter Sports

Everyone thinks the North Pole is a cold and gloomy _place_

at the top of the _earth_. Not true! Those of us who live here

all year round know that it's an awesome playground. There are

the usual winter activities, such as snowshoe _tag_, which

requires a fuzzy tennis _ball_ and a super long _stick_

to compete. Meanwhile, the younger folk play Ring Around the

rosie and Stick the _nose_ on the Snow _man_.

Of course, you do have to be sure you bundle up; it helps to wear

a thick, woolly _coat_ or two under your down _below_.

It can get a little crazy around here in December, too. Sometimes

we help the Post-moose-ter General sort each handwritten

letter sent to this address—they come by the bagful! But it

quiets down soon after the twenty-fifth, and we can all get back to

our favorite _holiday_ sports!

BONUS: Can you find the hatchet and wishbone?

Art by Mark Corcoran

Holiday Treats

We spent all day helping in the kitchen. We flattened out yards

and yards of _cookie_ dough and cut out dozens and dozens

of _sugar_ cookies. When they had baked and cooled, we

put them on sheets of waxed _paper_ and decorated them

with multicolor _sparkale_ sprinkles and _royal_ icing. We

also stirred crunchy _corn_ flakes into a bowl of creamy

cookie butter, and then rolled the mixture into the goodies

our family calls "No-Bake _candy_ Supremes." But all the

effort was worth it when we got a sweet reward afterward! We

were sitting by the blazing _fire_ enjoying some samples of

our handiwork when we heard chirping. We'd almost forgotten!

So we took the big bag of _bird_ seed outside and filled up

the _bird feeder_ hanging on the old oak tree. Why shouldn't our

feathered friends have a special _holiday_ treat today too?

BONUS: Can you find the boot, muffin, slice of pie, ice-cream cone, crayon, mushroom, shoe, and hockey stick?

Art by Linda Weller

Cactus Christmas

If you live in the hot, dry, dusty _desert_, it's easy to forget that

it's the holiday season. Since we couldn't find a traditional evergreen

tree, Francine Fox looked for the tallest _cactus_ in the

area, and we all pitched in to decorate it. Each colorful twinkling

light, sparkly _bulb_, and glittering _star_

really made it festive! You have to be careful, though. An ultrasharp

wrapping paper got stuck in my foot and had to be removed with

a plumber's _phone_. Ouch! Sammy Snake put on his Santa

hat to hand out the gifts. But then he remembered that he

didn't HAVE any hands, so Gomer Gopher and Francine took over.

We all gathered around and sang, "O cactus tree, o _cactus_

tree, how beautiful your _lights are_!" So you see, just because we

don't get piles of cold, wet, slushy _snow_ in the Southwest

doesn't mean that we don't know how to be merry!

BONUS: Can you find
the button, fishhook, and pennant?

Art by Neil Numberman

All I Want ...

For the entire year, I had been begging Mom and Dad for my very

own _cat_. I promised that I would take full responsibility,

and be sure to fill its _bowl_ with fresh _food_ every

day. I would give it only the best _time_ to play with, and I

would even brush its _hair_! My parents were not convinced.

"Wouldn't you rather have a five-speed _car_?" they asked.

"Or maybe a pair of pro-_motion_ skates? Even a three-wheeled

bike would be more fun." No matter what I said, they kept

shaking their heads. But someone WAS listening to me and thought

I was trustworthy enough. When I came downstairs on Christmas

morning, I heard a strange _meow_ coming from one of the

packages under the tree. I carefully lifted the _box top_ off the

box, and a small, furry _head_ popped up. And I've known all

year what I'm going to name it: _wish_!

BONUS: Can you find the tack, snake,
fishhook, nail, needle, ruler, crown, and button?

Art by Maxim Mitrofanov

Sleigh Ride

"Over the _____ and through the _____ to

Grandmother's house we go!" we sang as we started our journey.

Unlike the rest of the classic song, though, we soon discovered

that our _____ did NOT know the way to carry the

_____ through the white and drifting _____—oh!

Instead, the confused _____ took a very wrong _____

and we wound up in a deep, muddy _____ about a mile

from Grandma's house. The song did get it right about "How the

_____ does blow!" I can confirm that it DOES sting the toes

and bite the _____ as over the ground we walked, up to our

elbows in the freezing _____. When we finally arrived, we

were all so exhausted that we fell asleep right at the dining room

table, before we even had a taste of Grandma's mouth-watering

_____ pie. But she did save some slices for us. Hurrah!

Not Even a Mouse?

You've heard that poem about what happens on the _____

before Christmas: "Not a creature was stirring, not even a

_____." Well, I have news for you. I discovered that not

only does a _____ stir, it also sings and dances! I had crept

downstairs early hoping to catch a glimpse of _____ Nick…

when what to my wondering _____ should appear, was NOT

a miniature _____ and eight tiny reindeer, but a long-tailed

_____ and its buddy harmonizing on "Jingle _____

Rock." And it wasn't visions of _____ plums dancing in my

head. Oh no! It was a whole conga line doing the _____

Hop! I have to say, I did laugh when I saw them, in spite of myself.

They must have heard me because they quickly scattered like the

_____ of a thistle. But as they dove out of sight, I called after

them, "Happy Christmas to all, and to all a good _____!"

BONUS: Can you find the needle?

We Gather Together

Our "family" holiday reunion is a little different than most—none

of us are actually related. Alex and I met on the New_____

City High School _____ team and quickly became

friends. Alex then introduced me to _____, who was his

next-door _____. She brought along Giselle, a fellow member

of the gymnastics squad. (You should see her do a one-handed

backward _____—wow!) Giselle also belonged to the Future

_____'s Club, where Buster was the chief _____ officer.

As for Homer . . . well, he just sat down one day at our crowded

_____ in the cafeteria and never left. One _____ led

to another, and soon we were all just hanging around together. We

started calling ourselves The _____ Family and promised to

hold this annual reunion. Each of us invites a new _____ along,

too, because who doesn't need one more _____?

BONUS: Can you find the shuttlecock, wrench, and olive?

Art by Mark Corcoran

My Wish List

I've been waiting 364 days for this! I began making my ___wish___

list on December 26 of last year. I checked each item as I stood in line

at GiGi's Ginormous ___holiday___ Store: the ___science___ set with

___big___ wheels? Check. The deluxe double-sided ___tic tac toe?___

Check. A polka-dotted ___ball___? Check. Santa seemed

surprised when I handed him the six-foot-long ___list___. Then

he looked closer. "What is the name next to each ___toy___?"

he asked. "The person it's for," I said. "My friend Zara's rechargeable

___phone___ broke, so she needs a replacement. My neighbor

Mr. O'___Neill___ was having trouble starting his ___car___ this

summer, so he needs a new one. And my Uncle Martin . . ."

"So none of the things written here are for you?" Santa asked.

"I have everything I want, thank you," I said. "But I might need a

sharper pencil and a longer ___list___ of paper for next year."

BONUS: Can you find the game piece and candle?

Come as You Are

Every year, I plan the most stupendously surprising surprise

_____ party. At the last minute, I invite my friends over and

tell them NOT to drop whatever they're doing. "Just do whatever

you're doing but do it at my _____," I say. Sarah had been

knitting a striped _____ to give to her aunt, so she gathered

up her _____ of yarn. Aisha brought her _____ craft

and her cute dog, _____. Griffin was in the middle of building

a tiny _____. (Though when it started melting on our

brand-new living room _____, Mom asked him to leave it

outside.) Patrick came over while still in his _____ slippers.

Luckily, Ian was just taking a batch of cookies out of the _____

when I called him, so we had a tasty treat to nibble on along with

the potful of hot _____ Rachel had just made. Actually, I don't

plan this party at all—it's a stupendously surprising _____ to

me too!

Art by Iryna Bodnaruk

Owls on Ice

Every family has its own holiday tradition, like stringing pieces of

puffed _____ to make a festive _____ or sharing a

three-layered sugar-glazed _____ topped with chopped

_____. But we Hoots don't like being cooped up indoors

all day. We always head to the local _____ rink to show off

some awesome skating skills. Each of my relatives glides around as

gracefully as a long-necked _____ on a smooth _____.

What a sight to see Cousin Hoorietta hold Cousin Hooward over

her _____ as she twirls around and around. Even Grandpa

Hoot can do a quadruple _____ with one _____ tied

behind his back. Unfortunately, I am the only _____ in the

bunch. As soon as I try to stand, I slip and fall like I just stepped on a

slimy _____ peel. Dad tells me I shouldn't feel bad about that.

"You're giving it your owl, and that's owl that matters," he says.

BONUS: Can you find the leaf, heart, pennant,
candle, green bean, and wishbone?

Hit the Slopes

Not too many people are aware of this, but Kris Kringle (or "The White-Bearded _man_," as his fans call him) is a top-ranked _sled_. He's so good, he could win the _gold_ medal for the freestyle _sking_ at the Winter Olympics! Comet, Dasher, and Prancer—who prefer snowboarding—aren't bad either. Comet rules on the half-_____, and is known for his 360-_____ frontside spin. Dasher can carve the curves on the parallel giant _____ like he's the grandmaster _____ at a wood-whittling contest. As for the tricky back-bend reverse _____-kick ollie, Prancer reaches new heights—it's as if someone has shot him out of a supersonic _____! But when it comes to showboating on the slopes, Kris K. still outperforms them all. If he ever decides to give up his _____ job at the _____ workshop, he could go pro!

BONUS: Can you find the carrot and banana?

Art by Brian White

Out of the Woods

While our friend Manuel was away, we were taking care of his dog,

sparky. His grandma was sick and his family was off visiting

her. When we went to his _street_ to walk the dog, we realized

that they had left in such a hurry that they hadn't even had time to

put up one single Christmas _tree_! So we asked Dad to cut

down the nicest _tree_ on our farm. We tied it to our little

red _truck_ with a strong _Bull_ and pulled it out of the

woods. My brother also picked some sprigs of _leaves_. We

found an extra _set_ of lights and some leftover ornaments,

and decorated as best we could. Then Manuel called to say his

grandma was feeling better and he would be coming home that day.

Won't he be surprised when he sees that top-hatted _snowmas_

waving its twiggy _arms_? We built it on his front _yard_

to welcome him back. 'Tis the _season_ to be jolly, after all.

Art by Charles Jordan

A Very Merry Band

After a sold-out cross-country _____, our band is back

in the recording studio to lay down some tracks for our new

_____. Our last one, "Christmas Rock," reached as high as

number eight on _____ Magazine's top 100 chart, and we

think this one will do even better. Since then, we've added Rudy

"Funky _____" Deerfield, the great bass guitarist, to the

group—the crowd loves him. "_____" McCupid, as always, is

on keyboards; his jamming is as sweet as the _____ filling in

a _____ doughnut. Ellie "Little Drummer Girl" Elfberg wildly

waves her _____ sticks around like a hungry _____

on Thanksgiving. Of course, The Big Man himself plays a wailing

_____ and sings the lead vocals, hitting each _____

note like a home-run king. Be sure to get our latest song collection,

which we're calling "Joy to the _____!"

BONUS: Can you find the crown and screwdriver?

Art by David Helton

41

Test Tubing

What are the odds? My buddies Kate and Kyle and I each got a

new _doughnut_ tube from our grandparents for Christmas! So

we took them all out for a test-drive on _mill_ Hill in Rapid

hershy Park. Soon we turned it into a three-way _slide_

contest to see who could come up with the goofiest moves.

We rode sitting backward, sideways, and lying facedown on our

face!. Then I tried it with one _____ up in the air.

Kyle zipped down while throwing a fat, squishy _____—at

me! Kate had her arms out wide, pretending she was a 747 jumbo

_____. When our other friend Ahmet stopped by, he came

up with an even better _____. So we each put together our

own frosty _____, and Ahmet helped set them up in the back

of our tubes. Then we did each silly _____ again—this time

with a snowy co-_____ along for the ride!

BONUS: Can you find the hose, comb, fork, banana,
crown, pennant, snake, bell, and spoon?

Art by Laura Ferraro Close

sunglasses

Up on a Rooftop

The first time I heard the magical ~~santa~~ _story_ of how Christmas

presents are delivered, I was a little skeptical. "We don't have a

fireplace," I said to my friend Izzy, who lives in the _house_ below

mine. "What will he slide down?" Izzy thought about it. "Maybe he

brings his own _Magic_ ?" she suggested. But I didn't believe that.

So we went on a search through every nook and _cranny_ of

our building. We took the _elevator_ to each floor to see if we

could find at least one _fireplace_. Nothing. We tested the clankety

Door escape that zigzags up the side of our twenty-two-story

Building We agreed that it didn't seem sturdy enough to support

a jolly but chubby _Man_. Finally, we discovered a dark, steep

ladder that led to a hatch in the _roof_. When we pushed

it open and climbed through, there it was: a brick _fireplace_ wide

enough for Santa and a whole sleigh full of gifts!

BONUS: Can you find the golf club and pushpin?

Art by Neil Numberman

Answers

▼Front Cover

▼Page 4

▼Page 6

▼Page 8

▼Page 10

▼Page 12

▼Page 14

▼Page 16

▼Page 18

Answers

▼Page 20

▼Page 22

▼Page 24

▼Page 26

▼Page 28

▼Page 30

▼Page 32

▼Page 34

▼Page 36

Answers

▼Page 38

▼Page 40

▼Page 42

▼Page 44

Tear out sticker sheet here.

838C-01 © Highlights for Children

A Day at the Beach
pages 4–5

The Perfect Tree
pages 6–7

Loco for Cocoa
pages 8–9

Choo-Choo on This
pages 10–11

Home Sweet Home
pages 12–13

A–Caroling We Go!
pages 14–15

Winter Sports
pages 16–17

Holiday Treats
pages 18–19

magnifying glass	mitten	spoon	frying pan	banana	mallet
dog bone	snake	toothbrush	ruler	bell	pencil
heart	bread	coat hanger	candy kiss	turtle	envelope
chef's hat	peanut	green bean	moon	game piece	yo-yo
saltshaker	magnifying glass	pennant	seashell	ring	canoe
necklace	flowerpot	key	pie	horseshoe	kite
saw	handbell	scissors	megaphone	pencil	toothbrush
	book	ring	ice-cream cone	sock	sailboat
cupcake	magic wand	saltshaker	doughnut	ruler	toothbrush
pie	lollipop	ice-cream cone	lighthouse	hockey stick	sock
bowling ball	orange	hockey stick	taco	toothbrush	ruler
wishbone	saw	bat	fish	drinking straw	ice-cream cone
crown	tape	ghost	snow cone	whale	elf's shoe
shoe	fireman's hat	scissors	lollipop	toaster	tent
teacup	canoe	wishbone	umbrella	crown	candle
flashlight	fish	toothbrush	sailboat	mug	spoon

Highlights

Hidden Pictures®

Highlights

Hidden Pictures®

Highlights

Hidden Pictures®

Highlights

Hidden Pictures®

Highlights

Hidden Pictures®

Highlights

Hidden Pictures®

Highlights

Tear out sticker sheet here.

838C-01 © Highlights for Children

Cactus Christmas
pages 20–21

All I Want...
pages 22–23

Sleigh Ride
pages 24–25

Not Even a Mouse?
pages 26–27

We Gather Together
pages 28–29

My Wish List
pages 30–31

Come as You Are
pages 32–33

Owls on Ice
pages 34–35

ladle	handbag	book	glove	lollipop	domino
artist's brush	cake	boot	hammer	mitten	banana
spatula	ring	lollipop	ladle	snail	mushroom
toothbrush	bowling ball	butterfly	teacup	umbrella	spoon
bowling pin	fish	banana	book	golf club	toothbrush
pencil	pizza	kite	teacup	vase	umbrella
boot	candle	tack	flag	pear	ring
sock	moon	saucepan	dragonfly	glass	horseshoe
traffic light	dinosaur	kite	drum	chess piece	flashlight
baby's rattle	pencil	crown	elephant	baseball bat	fish
bird	ladder	bowl	flag	dinosaur	top hat
boat	ice-cream cone	beet	sock	ring	moon
envelope	pyramid	apple	snake	eggplant	crown
pear	baseball bat	key	ruler	fork	bell
canoe	teacup	chili pepper	frying pan	trowel	envelope
gravy boat	elf's shoe	bell	building block	artist's brush	boomerang

Highlights™
Hidden Pictures®

Hit the Slopes
pages 36–37

Out of the Woods
pages 38–39

A Very Merry Band
pages 40–41

Test Tubing
pages 42–43

Up on a Rooftop
pages 44–45

Tear out sticker sheet here. ✂

838C-01 © Highlights for Children

Write your own silly sticker story! Use markers to create your own stickers.

artist's brush	worm	envelope	heart	ladle	pie
cane	pear	feather	bell	seashell	doughnut
pushpin	cake	bell	pie	mallet	nail
pencil	artist's brush	ice-cream cone	ballpoint pen	golf club	candle
seashell	lemon	bread	golf club	necktie	chili pepper
puzzle piece	sailboat	leaf	sock	pencil	flowerpot
muffin	bird	watch	cloud	teacup	butterfly
feather	oar	ice-cream bar	lollipop	golf ball	musical note
skateboard	cupcake	flashlight	toothbrush		
comb	ice-cream cone	harmonica	paintbrush	paper airplane	hammer

Highlights™

Hidden Pictures®